disc

HOW DID THEY BUILD THAT?
HOW DID THEY BUILD THAT?
HOW DID THEY BUILD THAT?
HOW DID THEY BUILD THAT?
HOW DID THEY BUILD THAT?
HOW DID THEY BUILD THAT?

HOW DID THEY BUILD THAT?

SKYSCRAPER

BY VICKY FRANCHINO

COMMUNITY CONNECTIONS
?

CHERRY
LAKE
Publishing

Published in the United States of America by Cherry Lake Publishing
Ann Arbor, Michigan
www.cherrylakepublishing.com

Content Adviser: Nancy Kristof
Reading Adviser: Cecilia Minden-Cupp, PhD, Literacy Consultant

Photo Credits: Cover and page 1, ©Lynn Watson, used under license from Shutterstock, Inc.;
page 5, ©Joao Virissimo, used under license from Shutterstock, Inc.; page 7, ©Peter Bowater/
Alamy; page 9, ©Chad McDermott, used under license from Shutterstock, Inc.; page 11,
©GoGo Images Corporation/Alamy; page 13, ©qaphotos.com/Alamy; page 15,
©Camerab/Dreamstime.com; page 17, ©Denis Dryashkin, used under license from
Shutterstock, Inc.; page 19, ©Anton Gvozdikov, used under license from Shutterstock, Inc.;
page 21, ©Frances A. Miller, used under license from Shutterstock, Inc.

LIBRARY OF CONGRESS CATALOGING-IN-PUBLICATION DATA
Franchino, Vicky.
  How did they build that? Skyscraper / by Vicky Franchino.
    p. cm.—(Community connections)
  Includes index.
  ISBN-13: 978-1-60279-485-6
  ISBN-10: 1-60279-485-5
  1. Skyscrapers—Juvenile literature.
  I. Title II. Title: Skyscraper. III. Series.
  NA6230.F73 2010
  690—dc22   2008045245

Cherry Lake Publishing would like to acknowledge the
work of The Partnership for 21st Century Skills. Please
visit *www.21stcenturyskills.org* for more information.

SKYSCRAPER

CONTENTS

HOW DID THEY BUILD THAT?

A HISTORY OF SKYSCRAPERS

Have you ever been in a big city? If so, you have probably seen a skyscraper. Skyscrapers are very tall buildings. They seem to touch the sky. The first skyscraper was built in Chicago in 1885. It was 10 floors high. Today, some skyscrapers have more than 100 floors.

Today, Chicago has many skyscrapers. The Hancock Center (middle) is one of the tallest skyscrapers in Chicago.

There are skyscrapers in many countries. It is almost like a contest to see who can make the tallest building! The Burj Dubai skyscraper in the United Arab Emirates is the world's tallest.

Construction of the Burj Dubai began in 2004. It reached its full height in 2009.

Are there any skyscrapers near your home? Guess how many floors each skyscraper has. How many people do you think each building can safely hold? You might be able to find this information online or at the library.

7

GETTING READY TO BUILD

There is a lot of work to do before building begins. **Architects** decide how the building will look. Some buildings are very plain. Others have many windows. Architects use computers to create different designs.

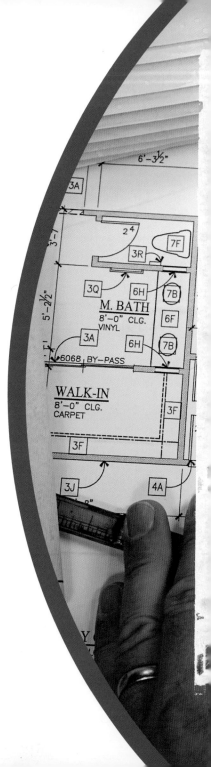

Architects used to draw all their plans by hand. Now they use computer programs to create designs.

Engineers make sure the building is safe and strong. They test **models**. The building must stand up against strong winds or earthquakes.

Other engineers decide where to put pipes and wires. Engineers also design the heating and cooling systems.

Architects and engineers work together. They make sure a building is built correctly.

LOOK!

Take a good look around your home. Look upstairs and downstairs. Look inside and outside. What are some things that an architect would decide? What would an engineer handle?

11

FROM THE GROUND UP

Foundations keep skyscrapers from sinking. Builders may also use **piles**. Piles are large posts that help support the weight of the building. Piles are formed by creating special holes in the ground. They are filled with **concrete**.

Piles go deep into the ground. They help support the skyscraper.

13

The **frame** holds up a skyscraper. The frame has **columns**. They go up and down. It also has **beams**. They run from side to side. The frame gives the skyscraper a shape the way your bones give your body its shape.

Frames can be made of steel and concrete. These make very strong frames. Triangles are strong shapes. Groups of many triangles are used in some frames.

14

Workers use a lift to help put steel beams in place.

Floors are made of steel and concrete. First, workers lay down steel. Then they pour concrete over it. The floor of one level is the ceiling for the level below.

Walls are added to the frame to make rooms. Some skyscrapers have many rooms. Others have just a few.

Windows will be placed in the openings in these walls.

17

Workers use **cranes** to lift building materials to upper floors. Sometimes helicopters are used!

The outside covering of the skyscraper is called cladding. Cladding can be made of many different things. Some skyscrapers are covered in glass. Others are covered with a type of metal called **aluminum**.

Cladding can be placed on lower floors while higher floors are still being built.

THINK!

Have you ever been inside a skyscraper on a windy day? Did you feel it move? Very tall buildings can bend slightly in the wind. Why do you think that is?

Working on a skyscraper can be dangerous. Workers must wear hard hats and special shoes. There are rules to follow when working in high places.

Look up the next time you see a skyscraper. Think about all of the work it took to build. Skyscrapers are amazing buildings!

Workers need to be extra careful when building a skyscraper.

GLOSSARY

aluminum (uh-LOO-mi-nuhm) a lightweight metal

architects (AR-ki-tektss) people who design buildings

beams (BEEMZ) long, thick pieces of metal or wood

columns (KOL-uhmz) long, vertical pillars

concrete (KON-kreet) material that hardens like stone and is made of cement, sand, gravel, and water

cranes (KRAYNZ) machines used to lift heavy things

engineers (en-juh-NIHRZ) people who help to plan and build a skyscraper

foundations (foun-DAY-shuhnz) the solid bases of buildings

frame (FRAYM) the part of a building that gives it shape

models (MOD-uhlz) small versions of things such as buildings

piles (PILEZ) large, heavy posts that are forced into the ground

FIND OUT MORE

BOOKS

Macken, JoAnn Early. *Building a Skyscraper*. Mankato, MN: Capstone Press, 2008.

Rau, Dana Meachen. *Skyscraper*. New York: Marshall Cavendish Benchmark, 2007.

WEB SITES

Big Apple History: Reaching for the Sky
pbskids.org/bigapplehistory/building/topic18.html
Read about some of New York's early skyscrapers

Building Big: The Skyscraper Challenge
www.pbs.org/wgbh/buildingbig/skyscraper/challenge/index.html
Find ways to fix some skyscraper problems with this fun activity

INDEX

ABOUT THE AUTHOR

Vicky Franchino has never visited the tallest building in the world, but she has visited the tallest building in the Americas: Willis Tower, fomerly known as the Sears Tower. Vicky lives in Madison, Wisconsin, with her husband and three daughters, and spends most of her days writing in her non-skyscraper, two-story house.

24